THE 'BREATH OF ODIN' AWAKENS

QUESTIONS & ANSWERS

THE 'BREATH OF ODIN' AWAKENS

QUESTIONS
&
ANSWERS

by
Frank A. Rúnaldrar

Part of the High Galdr Series
Questions & Answers
www.highgaldr.com/qa

Published in 2017 by:
Bastian & West
www.bastianandwest.com

Part of High Galdr Series Questions & Answers
www.highgaldr.com/qa

ISBN: 978-0-9955343-1-5

A CIP catalogue record for this book is available from the British Library.

Cover design adapted by Bastian & West from original by Judge a Cover Designs.
Book typeset in Niva Light by PeGGO Fonts, Norse font by Joël Carrouché and runic elements in Felt-Tip Futhark by Thomas Kaeding.

I would like to take the opportunity to thank all my readers, both for their interest and their contributions. For those I have had the pleasure to converse with – it has been a privilege; one I hope to repeat.

TABLE OF CONTENT

APPENDIX

Preface

This Q & A tackles a number of highly relevant questions received from readers of 'The Breath of Oðin Awakens'[1] (BoD). The most interesting ones have been selected for further discussion, deepening theoretical and practical understanding, as well as introduce new complimentary practices.

GENERAL QUESTIONS

1. I'M STRUGGLING FEELING THE HEAT OF ᚠ Fé (Fehu)?

This is common when starting these types of practices. One of the key things to remember is that when you do them initially, you are relying on imagination to guide you to the actual energy of ᚠ Fé (Fehu). By imagining something over and over again you set your spirit and mind to vibrate in synergy with what you are imagining. On the spiritual and mental levels the principle: '*like attracts like*' applies, as a result what can be termed a harmonic resonance in between the spirit/mind and the energy sought is established. This then puts you in touch with the real runic energy rather than the imagined.

How does this work in practice? Well, you start of by relaxing and letting the world fade from your immediate awareness. This puts you into an alpha brainwave pattern which results in a light trance. Entering into this type of relaxed trance will loosen (but not separate) the spirit from the limitations of the flesh. Providing you have become sufficiently relaxed, your conscious awareness will stop registering things around you. You will experience a shift of spiritual (hence also mental) focus; a type of release from the tensions of the world. This is where you need to work from when approaching runic energies.

In the forthcoming publications, we will look at many methods to speed this process up. For the time being, simply taking a few breaths, letting go of the worries of the world, and willing the tense parts of your body to relax is a quick yet highly effective way of achieving the needed trance state.

When you reach your relaxed trance, the next step is to imagine yourself sitting in an endless universe with no up, no down, no left, no right. Just you sitting in an infinite expanses of emptiness all around you. Doing this will pull you into a slightly deeper trance and will further shift your focus away from the physical. Once settled in this state of mind, the trick is to utter out loud the rune ᚠ Fé (Fehu), chant it over and over again if need be. As you do, visualise its shape around you or in-front of you. Each time you chant the rune's name imagine its red hot fiery energy exploding outwards in all directions. Feel the heat on your skin, see the red energy all around you and hear 'Feeeejeh' (or if using the Germanic form: 'Fehuuuuuu') as it echoes outwards. After a couple of chants, you should be seeing yourself at the centre of a massive fiery universe expanding so far out that you cannot perceive a starting or ending point.

It is important to just relax and enjoy this fiery universe, seeing it, feeling it and hearing it. After you have done so a few times, calling forth the energy of ᚠ Fé (Fehu) should become quicker and easier!

With practice, you will find that all you need to do is to utter the rune's name and without even trying to, you will feel the heat and see the vast red power expanding all over the place. When this starts to happen automatically and it just manifests of its own accord when you utter the rune, you have hit the jackpot. At that point, you are dealing with the real power of ᚠ Fé (Fehu) and not the imagined. What you would have done here is used imagination to propel yourself into the real current of the rune.

This is also where caution is needed. During the phase where you worked with imagined ᚠ Fé (Fehu) no harm could come (as it was imagined, hence not real). When you start working with real ᚠ Fé (Fehu), energy overloading can cause all sorts of problems. For this reason, when you are moving from the imaginary to actually using ᚠ Fé (Fehu) energy in your Hamingja work, start slowly. It is good practice to start with 3 breaths, and move 9 gradually by increasing the number by only 1 each time. In this manner your energy body, your physical and your spiritual all get used to the new increase of power gradually. When using fire runes and overdoing it, you are in danger of burning out micro-channels in the energy body. These take a very long time to heal (20 to 40 years). For this reason, it is advised to proceed slowly and take it one step at a time.

Always remember to move all the ᚠ Fé (Fehu) energy out of the physical body and INTO the Hamingja. Otherwise you will miss out on the hamingja boost, which is the goal of this work, and you will run the risk of developing physiological side-effects, such as increased body temperature, tendency to dehydrate

and so forth. Slow and steady is the master key!
Better safe than sorry.

2. IN SOME PRACTICES YOU INCLUDE RUNE ENERGY SENSATIONS AND COLOURS BUT NOT IN OTHERS?

Although this might at first be somewhat confusing it is done deliberately. Where there are no colours and sensations described in the text, you should just use either the Germanic or Icelandic rune names, instead of full Galdr (which is used when the colours and sensations are added to the rune name chants). The reason for this is simply to avoid exposing your Hamingja, physical and energy bodies to more energy than they can handle. Using a simple runic name chant will allow you to connect loosely with the energies of that rune instead of working directly with its full force. This prevents overloads, which can cause a lot of damage when working with the Önd (Breath of Oðin) and the Hamingja. If you absolutely need to visualise a colour for runes which do not have one specified use the traditional one: red.

Once you have worked through and integrated the full Self, it is at that point safe to unleash full

Galdr in this type of practice. You are building the resistance of your Self to higher concentrations of energy and power. Think of it as a gradual stretching and strengthening of the Self which enables it to deal with a grater amount and intensity of energy.

3. Do you practice these too? Do I need to practice all of these daily? How often should I practice? For how long?

Absolutely, without fail. So much so that if I am so busy and lack the time to do them I will skip lunch to do them (which I do not recommend others do by any means!).

They have become such a routine practice that skipping it altogether is not something I would want to do. On the plus side, once you have worked through all the stages there is no need to repeat them all. I keep my routine going with Stage 2 and Stage 6 daily (these can found at p.37 and p.74 in the BoO[1]). Stage 2 is pretty much needed to keep safe, and Stage 6 is the final completion of all the work you do from 1 to and including Stage 6. This is a rather good point to keep in mind otherwise it would be extremely time consuming to repeat all of the practices up to an including Stage 6. Stage 7 (found at p.89 in the BoO[1]) I only use when I do rune work which is definitely not on a daily basis (unfortunately).

As it happens quite a few of us on the production team for this book have taken up doing these on a regular basis. Different people derive different benefits from these exercises and when they do they very quickly stick to them.

4. I'M STRUGGLING WITH ICELANDIC NAMES, CAN I USED THE GERMANIC ONES AND GET THE SAME RESULTS?

Absolutely. The rule of thumb is to use whichever system of naming works best for you. Ultimately you will move from both of these to the actual phonetic sound of the runes. The reason for focussing on the Icelandic is that it contains the phonetics in the actual names for all the runes so the shift is a little easier to make than it is for some of the runes when pronounced in their Germanic equivalents.

The only exception to the rule is the rune ᛃ Ár (Jera). In this case, the actual phonetics are preserved in the Germanic rune name rather than the Icelandic.

5. Do I need to worship Odin to do this right?

Short answer no. When reading the text closely, you can see that the Gods and Goddesses are not really mentioned in any of the practical materials nor are they relied on in any of the methods. The primary reason is simply that the Gods do not like to be called 'willy nilly' for any odd thing. Constant stream of prayers, demands, general chit chat is considered to be a reflection of weakness in spirit and personality and goodness knows how they dislike weakness.

From a mythology point of view, we are shown how mankind is given many tools, imbued with powers and taught with the knowledge of the Gods. Mankind is positively empowered to fend for itself without having to go asking for one thing after another like an annoying child who refuses to learn to do things for him or herself. Remember the Gods are all warriors, in some shape or form. Even the Goddess of Love, Freya, is a warrior Goddess; as well as constantly battling the 'empty' (which is the actual meaning of the word: chaos) in order to preserve creation.

There is no room for weakness, there is no excuse for not fighting over and over again. It is only once you have exhausted all possible resources available to you and come to the absolute end of every possible course of action, only when there is absolutely nothing else you can do, that you should ever ask. We are embodiments of the divine, each and every one in our own way and capacity.

6. I'M A CHRISTIAN CAN I
USE THIS STUFF TOO?

Yes, you can. Remember before the forceful conversion to Christianity, most if not all Europeans followed the Old Norse ways. Irrespective of what your current belief (or disbelief) systems are now, the Old Norse is in our DNA, our blood and our heritage.

As you will have noticed the mysticism side of things is focused on runes and general cosmic principles and has very little (if any) interaction with the Norse Gods themselves. It follows therefore that effectively you are working with universal principles. It is possible to do all the practices without getting involved with the Norse Gods as long as you do not start linking the underlying principles to the Christian pantheon and theological principles. A tradition mix-mash can strip the effectiveness of the underlying principles at work.

My advice would be if you want to use this as a Christian stick to a pure spiritual view when working with it and avoid tainting it with Christian religious concepts and it should work perfectly fine. Getting familiar with the Norse cosmology will help and prove essential in later work.

Another point to consider is that in Iceland the old tradition (Norse) is combined (and used in parallel) with the Christian and the two have co-existed for a very long time. There are many crossing points in-between both traditions' theologies. For instance, in the Christian one God is said to have created the universe by saying *'Let there be light'* and creation exploded forth. In runic mysticism, that is EXACTLY what the rune master/mystic does. He uses the universal language (the runes) to create and shape reality. There are many such parallels in between the two theologies to be found.

7. DOES EVERYONE HAVE A HAMINGJA?

That is debatable. Some people give theirs away, others entrust theirs to third parties and some are believed not to have any in the first place. According to the Saga of Ríg[2], Heimdall gives his name and hence Hamingja to his son Ríg who is the first Jarl. There is no mention of a gift of Hamingja during the initial creation of Ask and Embla (first man and woman) by the holy trinity (Oðin, Húnir and Lóðurr) which would mean that the Hamingja is only available to those who are descendants of the original Jarls or Gods which have subsequently bestowed them upon their descendants.

However, I have yet to meet anyone without one who has not given his/hers away. When looking at a person's energy body it is painfully obvious that they have a Hamingja and even when they gift theirs you can still see the link to it during their lifetime. So either we are missing some of the records of mass bestowing of Hamingja by the original Jarls and Gods (which is highly likely) or somehow future generations have all managed to acquire one.

It is important to keep in mind that having a Hamingja and having a powerful one are two completely different things. There are those who are literally in possession of a blinding sun and those in whom it is only vaguely noticeable. Not all Hamingja are equal! Actually, no two I have seen have ever been alike let alone identical.

My personal theory is that the Hamingja reflects the individualisation of the Self, and since we are ultimately all totally unique as we become more and more individualised the same runs true for our Hamingja.

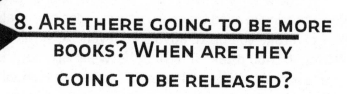

8. Are there going to be more books? When are they going to be released?

Absolutely. We are all working hard to get a number of additional titles in the High Galdr series out. Many of you have also asked if we could reveal ahead of time what subject would be covered next and when they will be made available. It is a pleasure to share some of the gems we have in store.

The process from conception to publication can be time consuming. First off, manuscripts need to prepared. Then, practices tested by people of each gender. Beyond that, manuscripts will be refined. This can be quite a daunting task in its own right. In general, taking into account both the generation of the materials, the testing phases and the refinement stages, it takes approximately one year to get the manuscript ready before submission to publication. Once ready, the publication process begins. I am told to plan in between six to eight months, by the ladies and gents involved, before the book is ready for print and public distribution.

Having said all of this, not to keep our readers waiting too long, we have implemented a system that allows us to work on each new title as soon as the manuscript for the previous title has been completed. This allows for time saving, and means that only a delay of around six months in-between book is expected.

For those of you who read at some speed, it is worth bearing in mind that each title includes materials that can take you up to advanced levels. As a rule of thumb, it should take anything between six months up to a year to master all the practices to a reasonably proficient level (with full mastery taking several years). In other words, the time it takes to work through the practices in each book is not far apart to the period needed to get the next title should be ready.

In order to give you all a bit of a taste of how the High Galdr series is structured:

- For those of you who read it, you will know that the first title 'The Breath of Oðin Awakens'[1] deals with the Hamingja and the Önd.

- The second book will look at the spirit, the mind and perceptions; better known as the Óðr (Odr), the Hugr and Minni. It will provide deep insights into the consciousness itself and how this spiritual level of the Self operates together with how we can make the most use of it!

- The third book will look at the physical and energetic level of the Self, this includes the physical body (Lik), the mysteries of blood, DNA, the energy body (which is akin to our blueprint, called the Hamr in Norse terminology, or etheric in modern day terminology) and the shadow Self (the Sal).

- The fourth book will look at the Fylgja (or Fetch as it is sometimes referred to). This title in combination with the Breath of Oðin Awakens will complete the archetypal level of the Self (see p.10 in the BoO[1]).

- Finally, the fifth book wraps all these teachings of the Self up and looks at their interactions, the merging and awakening of the Spark of Self, which eventually leads to the awakening of the Divine Spark (or rather the shifting of a Spark of the Self into a Divine Spark). This title provides the final guidance and skill sets required to unleash actual Galdr, in other words High Galdr.

- The sixth book provides invaluable teachings on actual High Galdr, its methods, its effects, how to use it, practices for unleashing it and most importantly how to target its effects on specific levels of the Self and / or reality.

- The seventh book in the series expands on this and looks at how High Galdr is used with runic combinations, bindrunes, runepathing and other specialised multiple rune practices. Technically, these last titles complete the series.

Due to high demand, we have however mapped out the exclusive release of an additional three books in addition and in parallel to the High Galdr series which focus singularly, and in some detail, on the sexual side of the Norse mysteries. One for men only, one for women only and one with additional materials for men and women. All three of these titles are supplementary and should be considered advanced materials. They do not form the part of the core-requirements for High Galdr.

Providing the series does well, we have also made provisions to publish several additional advanced self-standing titles which will be announced when the time is right. Please do keep in mind that the outline shared with you is an outline only, and can change prior to publication. It should not be by any means considered finalised.

The important thing to keep in mind is that the High Galdr series have been structured to start by providing the knowledge and practices needed to master and understand your Self in every possible sense of the term. The manner of setting out is intended to facilitate organic advancement and empower you to become proficient in Galdr. This is why most mystery schools over the ages have always had the saying '*Know Thyself*' as the starting point for all students. It is why the core of the subject matter is left to the point where the Self has at least become familiar territory. Between the first five books, all the required skills are covered. Without mastering them Galdr will not be effective and prove to be more of a hit and miss success rather than have the actual punch it has.

HEALTH, HEALING
&
SPORTS QUESTIONS

9. CAN MEGIN BE USED FOR HEALING? I'M A HEALER HOW CAN I USED THIS FOR HEALING ?

Absolutely, yes! Self-healing is one of the default functions of Megin. Much like an automatic system - if there is anything to heal, Megin will be used first and foremost for that purpose. This applies not only to the physical body (Lik) but also to other parts of the psycho-spiritual Self. Using Megin to heal others however is a very complex field. It would not be an overstatement to say that a number of books could be written on the topic and they would still not capture the entirety of such healing practices. Due to limited space we cannot go into all the detail at this stage, and serve to leave you with some common examples and give you an outline that can be adapted to suit specific needs.

First of all, you will need to research the condition you are looking to heal. It goes without saying that the approach will vary greatly depending on the condition in question. For example, dealing a broken bone or a fever would be very different to dealing with a personality disorder. Much like there are different treatment methods in medicine for different conditions, the same applies to runic healing with Megin.

In this outline we will avoid dealing with the medical aspect and go straight to the runic side of things (but always pursue the medical). Runic healing should compliment the medical field's work and not replace it. At least not at this stage of spiritual development of the Ætts (Clans).

Personality Disorders

Personality disorders typically arise due to some type of disharmony at a spiritual level of the Self and propagate to the other levels. For instance, a Hugr which is at odds with a Minni and working against the Fylgja can result in multiple personalities. They can also arise in consequence of some form external interference (for example, when another actor is influencing the person's mind). This scenario is far less frequent but should not be discarded as one of the options. For those with clairvoyant sight, it is simply a matter of looking at the individual's energy body (the Hamr) and shadow body (Sal) and see if any patterns which do not match those of the Self are being superimposed upon them. If so, it is an eternal mind at play. If not, it is an internal issue.

When trying to re-harmonises warring parts of the Self, the runes to use for the physical level which includes the energy body and shadow are M Eykur (Ehwaz) and P Vin (Wunjo) together and at the same time, or M Eykur (Ehwaz) and F Óss (Ansuz) for the spirit level (including the mental). When attempting to rid someone of an intrusive 'thing', the runes to use are ᚺ Hagall (Hagalaz) and ᛋ Sól (Sowilo) together followed by ᚦ Þurs (Thurisaz) and ᛋ Sól (Sowilo), and finally the ᛈ Vin (Wunjo) and ᚠ Óss (Ansuz) runes. The first pair of runes work on the physical, the second on the spiritual and the third on the archetypal levels of the Self; covering all the fundamental bases.

Bones, Muscles and Nervous System

For breakages in bones, ᛈ Óðal (Othala) and / or ᛁ Íss (Isa) energy should be used and driven straight into the injured area (in the case of broken bones, the applicable broken bone once it has been medically set (otherwise they could heal wrong, faster but still wrong). For muscular issues, the rune ᚢ Úr (Uruz) makes for an obvious choice and for nervous system issues the ᛞ Dagur (Dagaz) rune in combination with the appropriate corrective rune. This selection of runes will cover most breakages and sprains situations.

General Practices

As you can see healing is indeed a very complex science. For general purposes two simple practices can be applied (but do keep in mind they are general).

The first requires you to step into the personalised Hamingja. From it, using its hands touch the physical body of the person you are treating and allow Megin to flow into the organ, tissue, mind, that which needs healing. Whilst doing this, will the Megin to repair and regenerate, then merge back into your physical. Follow this up with an empowered runic

27

uttering (see Stage 7, p.89 in the BoO[1]) of either the ᚢ Úr (Uruz) rune (if repairing), the ᚠ Óss (Ansuz) to harmonise the mental level (if working on a mental issue) or the ᚹ Vin (Wunjo) rune if harmonising the physical level.

The second method can be used when the patient is not too poorly and has energy reserves of his or her own left to manipulate. In this case, all you need to do is to utter the relevant rune and make that energy flow along the body of the patient INTO their Hamingja with the clear intent that it should be used to generate the appropriate type of Megin for healing and direct it as the body sees fit for healing. This method relies a bit more on the patient's own Self but tends to be far more effective since it will know exactly what needs to be done. The healer will do no more than provide the resources needed and will the job to be done; effectively triggering the healing process, with healing following suit.

These two approaches should give you a solid general set of tools to work with.

10. I'M AN ATHLETE USING THE TECHNIQUES IN HERE I HAVE NOTICED MY RECOVERY FROM PHYSICAL EXERCISE GREATLY SPEEDING UP?

This is not surprising. In fact, technically speaking, it is precisely what should happen. The default behaviour of the Hamingja is to produce Megin which is then primarily used for (1) healing of the body, (2) weaving the Ørlǫg (fluctuating fate of the individual, personal path through life) and (3) bringing success to endeavours where luck is needed or any form of competition is involved; in that order. Once you fill the Hamingja, any spare Megin will automatically be used to heal. This explains why this is described as the 'default' position. You do not need to do anything other than make sure there is sufficient Megin in it for this to happen. It is only once the healing has completed that any spare Megin is used for other purposes. This is also why people who are not careful and just spill their Megin left right and centre run into health issues and / or start to age very quickly. A shortage prevents the body from repairing properly and deteriorative qualities will therefore become visible.

Turning to the crux of the question, and how post exercising recovery can be optimised using Megin, the best way to do this is to fill the Hamingja with additional ᚠ Fé (Fehu) (or ᚢ Úr - Uruz) energy as soon as possible post exercise. Give it about 10 minutes after you have filled it and focus on the Hamingja sitting at the back of your shoulder blades. From there, feel the Megin (in most people it is a type of cool electric sensation, often a type of vibrant light blue) flowing into the muscles and literally bathing them in Megin whilst focusing on the intent for them to recover faster and faster or stronger and stronger (as appropriate). When doing this, always stick to one goal. If you start with one goal, then another, then another and another, your Hamingja will get awfully confused. It will either make a mess of it or do nothing. It is far more effective to stick with the one goal in each, setting and waiting until that is done. Keep in mind you are communicating with the body's nervous system which is not able to deal with logic, complex matters or anything outside of its scope. Those matters are for your conscious awareness and the Hugr not the Lik (body) or the Hamr. Remember to stick to the scope of the functions for each part of the Self. Moving away from that will create disharmony and conflict.

You will have noted the rune ᚢ Úr (Uruz) mentioned above. There is a good reason why. This is one of the runes of healing and of physicality, indirectly also involved in shaping the Hamr. It can be used to speed up recuperation. If your objective is faster recovery, speedier regeneration, and prompt healing, then ᚢ Úr (Uruz) is your rune. If however you are looking to boost strength and power, then ᚠ Fé (Fehu) is your rune.

You may ask, how does one use ᚢ Úr (Uruz)? The answer is simple. In exactly the same way as ᚠ Fé (Fehu) (using the exercise described above in answer to question 1) but changing the sensations and visuals as well as the rune name to be pronounced to ᚢ Úr (Uruz). It will result in a lighter green energy (think grass green as sunlight passes over it). The sensation is one of weight or mobile/fluid earth with a hint of warmth to it (like mud); here think of grabbing a handful of soil in your hand and letting it fall from in between your fingers. That substance of soil, mass and solidity, yet also its flexibility is exactly what ᚢ Úr (Uruz) energy feels like. It will have weight but it is not immovable solid dense, and the name to use is naturally ᚢ Úr (Uruz)! Once you have reached the point where these sensations, visuals and sounds just manifest automatically without having to be imagined you are ready to use ᚢ Úr (Uruz) energy to fill your Hamingja with. This will produce a slightly different type of Megin which will have a tint of solidity to it which the ᚠ Fé (Fehu) type does not have. This type of Megin is distinguishable by a sensation of cool electric gel-like substance.

All that remains is to channel it as you would do with the ᚠ Fé (Fehu) into the target area/muscle(s) and will it (or direct it) to heal and boost the self-regeneration process. If you have got to the stage where you have formed your personalised Hamingja (see Stage 3, p.42 in the BoO[1]) the process is slightly different. The change you will need to make is to breath in the runic energy directly into the person-ified Hamingja. In effect, you are breathing through it rather than through your physical body. Then the same process applies as given above (channelling to the directed area/muscle(s)) except that the Megin generated is channelled through the hands of the personified Hamingja rather than from the patch of the back (see Stage 3, p.43 in the BoO[1]).

If you are skilled in using the personified Hamingja, there is a shortcut you can take advantage of. It involves breathing the runic energy into the personified Hamingja, then once the Megin begins to flow, move it inside the Hamingja's form to where you want it in the physical. For instance, if you want to heal the calf muscles move it into the lower portion of the legs of the Hamingja's form and concentrate it there. Then all you need to do is step with the personified Hamingja into the physical, maintaining awareness in both as you did during the practices outlined in the BoO[1]. As the two forms are identical and the Megin spills from Hamingja to the physical, you will flood the calf muscles with highly concentrated Megin and activate it in both the muscle fibres as well as the blood flowing into and out of the muscle (remember the discussion regarding Megin flowing through blood and activating DNA?). It takes some practice but doing it this way is a very quick and effective way of targeting very specific physical locations without having to make the Megin flow out of the Hamingja down the body until it reaches the desired location (in other words the Megin is localised directly in the required area and need not travel around the body until it reaches the right area).

11. Since starting these, about three weeks in, I've noticed less need to use my inhalers for my asthma. After a month or so I've practically stopped using it?

Interestingly, this has been reported by more than one reader, alongside loss of allergies, alleviation of a few other long term conditions (which due to the request not to and respect of privacy of the individuals involved we cannot detail). Before continuing, a word of caution, to be responsible and remember that your doctor should be kept in the loop of your health condition at all times. Even in cases where improvement is found, changes in medication should only ever be directed, managed and supervised by your doctor.

On the mystical / Megin side of things, self-healing is to be expected. As mentioned previously the Hamingja and Megin produced will primarily by default have a regenerative effect on both the body (Lik) and other parts of the Self. For long term or more complex health conditions, this can be very gradual. In other words, the improvements can happen but will feel like a tiny step at a time rather than the instant effect typically expected. For diseases which are part of our Ørlǫg, healing is far more difficult and time consuming. Nonetheless, it can happen. The trick is to keep an eye out on the underlying condition and monitor it as you practice. For some people these long-term health conditions have become so foundational that the healing can be extremely disruptive in its own right. In such cases, it might be best to take it slow and focus the Megin by will and intent to be directed first at other parts of the Self which should smooth things out a little. Be sensible about all this, if it becomes difficult to manage and the effects of the practices are disruptive, that is a sign to slow down! Listen to your body, it is your foundation and key for everything...

JOBS, MONEY
&
WEALTH QUESTIONS

12. How can I use this to get rich?

The good old question of getting a quick foot into massive wealth. Before we move onto how to increase the likelihood and affinity for wealth let us get one thing straight: this practice will not allow you to make millions of millions overnight. All it will do is increase the flow the wealth available to you.

There are two main runes to use for a wealth boost. They are ᚠ Fé (Fehu) and ᚱ Reið (Raidho). Start off by uttering the ᚠ Fé (Fehu) rune (as outlined in BoO[1] Stage 7, vocalisation practice, p.89). Allow its energy to spill all over the town, country, earth, as far as possible. Imbue it with the intent that it carries wealth. Then, use the ᚱ Reið (Raidho) rune. Utter it at your feet and see it spider out threads in all directions. Will them to build the pathways for wealth carried by the ᚠ Fé (Fehu) energy towards you. See it flowing through the pathways established by ᚱ Reið (Raidho) towards you, then up your legs and throughout your body. Next will it to flow out of the body into your aura and stay there pulsating outwards pulling more and more wealth towards you.

This simplified form of runic weaving will over several practices increase the flow of wealth and circumstances which lead to earning more. How the money actually gets to you will depend entirely on the pathways already available. If you run a business, you might see increase in customers, run into offers to do some extra work, or be given a bonus. To maximise on wealth opportunities, avoid closing any possible avenues. This will lead to more conduits for wealth to flow back to you, even possibly along multiple pathways simultaneously!

13. If there a way that I can use the Megin to improve my job hunting chances?

A very practical question. Yes, you can. There are two ways to do so and I suggest using both.

The first step is relatively easy and involves regularly increasing the amount of Megin in your Hamingja (see Stages 1, 4 and 6 of the BoO[1], pages 28, 57 and 74). This will automatically boost your chances in whatever you do. Remember, when job hunting you are COMPETING against all other applicants. Since this is a competition Megin comes into play automatically and is at the forefront of things. Keep charging up and stay as full as possible.

The second step is a more active one. There are a few things you can do to further increase your chances of success: by imbuing your CV with Megin, by building up a ᚠ Fé (Fehu) and ᛟ Óðal (Othala) Megin boosted 'auric field' (or as scientists term it a 'personal bacterial cloud') and by flooding your visualisations with it.

In this day and age, imbuing your CV can be a somewhat limited option. Thanks to technology, the use of paper based CVs with cover letters in a job application process has become nearly redundant, replaced by computerised applications. Arguably, a pretty deliberate move to strip the diversity of human expression out and replace it with 'perfectly predictable' numbers and behaviours. In some sectors and at some levels, not least high profile jobs, forms and CVs are still common, and this technique can be used in this scenario.

For those of you who still find it relevant, complete your form or CV, have the paper copy in front of you. Relax. Vocalise the ᚠ Fé (Fehu) and ᚱ Reið (Raidho) runes, one after the other whilst focussing on the intent that you will get the job and take the path of least resistance to it! Will the energy from the vocalisation to flow down your arms as you hold the paper and into the paper. Lock it there by willing it to exert its 'effects, stronger and strong, until I get the job'. Then either send it on, or hand it into whoever needs to take hold of it.

To effect yourself and increase the chances of getting the job you will have to cause your auric field to attract the desired job and combine this with a shift of perception at the interview stage. This will make the interviewers see you as the best possible candidate for the position. You could also do the inverse and make the others seem like the worst pick but since you would have to be in their presence this will seldom be practical. For those ethically motivated, remember the Norse tradition is a warrior tradition and getting a job today is a battle indeed!

To get this done, you will need to have first mastered Stage 7 (p.89) in the BoO[1]. Use that practice to utter the following runes in this order: ᛉ Óðal (Othala), ᚠ Fé (Fehu) then ᛈ Vin (Wunjo) and pull their energy into your aura by visualising the actual runes radiating from your body into the auric field. Will the energy to make you more and more in tune with the job, that everyone who gets close to you immediately comes to the realisation that you are the best person for the job. That it is a perfect fit for you and you for it. Will this runic energy to keep radiating over and over again until you have obtained the job. Follow this by the ᚱ Reið (Raidho) one. This time see it radiating out of you, and pulling you towards the job. It leaves a trail or path or road which you are walking on right into the job, guiding you to the desired job. For the theorists, the first three runes act inwards, pulling attention to you, then ᚱ Reið (Raidho) acts as an outwards flow guiding you into the job. This bi-directionality leads to direct manifest-ation and harmonisation of the inwards with the outwards flow. This is an advanced runic technique called 'pathing'. The complete use of it is a little more complex, but for now, its simplified form will do the trick.

The final option is to increase the chances of success in obtaining the actual job in the first place. Besides using the above given runes in the described way you can also shift into the personified Hamingja. Putting its hands on your shoulders, will a stream of Megin to flow from it all over your body. As you do, see yourself doing the job you are after. Will it to be so. For those few moments whilst the energy

43

is flowing visualise that YOU ARE doing that job. IT IS YOUR JOB. Then return to your daily activities and AVOID thinking about what you have just done. This, combined with the above and the simplified pathing will provide you with a considerable advantage!

QUESTIONS ON
ADVANCED TOPICS
&
THEORIES

14. Post circulation there seems to be less Megin but it seems to have thickened, what's happening?

A very astute observation! What is happening is simply the Megin coalescing and gaining more substance. This type of thickening can be thought of as a solidification or materialisation of Megin. In other words, it is becoming more concentrated. A concentration typically occurs because of multiple 'thickening' events in its substance.

The good news is that this is exactly what you should be aiming for. The less subtle the Megin, the more punch it gains. Additionally, since it is now more concentrated, you can have a much larger store of it as well and a more pronounced effect on the physical and energetic realities.

This is a good practical example of the 'spirit taking on matter' principle and becoming something more than it originally was. As for the use of concentrated

Megin, the groundwork is still the same. The only change you will notice is that you will need less of it to produce an effect. The other thing to be mindful of is not to overuse the Megin in a single application. If you previously needed say 3 breaths of Megin to fill your runic vocalisation, you should reduce it to 1 and observe the effectiveness of it. Then if need be increase to 2, and so forth until you get a measure of the number of breathes needed.

15. Can I used the Breath of Oðin without working with the hamingja? Can I work with the hamingja without bothering with the breath?

An interesting and tricky question! At this stage of spiritual human evolution, regrettably the answer is no.

The Breath of Oðin (Önd) is the flowing Megin throughout the various parts of the Self. For the Megin to flow it needs to be produced natively within the Self and that is the function of the Hamingja. The reason for limiting the answer to 'this stage of spiritual human evolution' is that at a later stage as we become more and more alike to the state of divinity it becomes possible. When you flow throughout creation you become part of the infinite unlimited flow of Megin which is present throughout creation. In other words, we become at one (take not of the 'at one' rather than 'one with', you are harmonising with not becoming one with), and Megin becomes part of us. As you have access to limitless Megin at the outset, there is no longer a need to produce it. However, in all cases, it is still desirable to maintain individualised Megin via personal production. The universal Megin supply method is one that the Gods and Goddesses have monopolised and sought to manipulate through time to gain the personal. When they came to a stumbling block, they tried to incarnate. Their aspiration to have a personal Megin has fuelled their appetite to incarnate in the first place (or so I am told). Their natural Önd is a little different to ours and cannot really in their context be translated as 'Breath of Oðin'. The underlying principles and modus operandi however is exactly the same, with the only difference being in its scope of functioning rather than mode of function.

From our current perspective it is best to think of the answer to this question as not possible, not yet. Besides, having the Hamingja and breath inter-functioning is essential to a number of key practical applications. As such, which it may be possible to separate them out theoretically and conceptually, it is not possible to separate them practically. For instance, practically all of the sexual mysticism and related practices would become impossible to practice without the Hamingja, as would the production of rune specific Megin individualised to your Self and so forth.

A most fascinating question resulting from deeper insight into the subject matter here. A delight to come across.

16. WHAT EXACTLY HAPPENS TO THE ENERGY BODY, THE ASTRAL AND SPIRITUAL WHEN WE CIRCULATE THE MEGIN AS EXPLAINED IN STAGE 6 PRACTICAL?

First off let us iron out a few definitions. Often when referring to the 'astral' body we find a whole range of different definitions as to what 'astral' actually is or refers to. So much so that it has resulted in a muddled perception of what could or could not be 'astral'. There are a number of debates as to whether the so-called astral actually even exists or whether it is all just an illusion or semi-illusion as most dreams are. Some define it as the emotional body, others as the light body, some as the dream body, some even confuse it with what is typically called the etheric body (in Norse terms the Hamr, energetic blueprint for the physical form), others confuse it with the mental body, some with the spirit body and so forth.

To avoid adding to the confusion, the response is limited to the actual known parts of the Self. The closest thing we have to an actual equivalent of an 'astral' body can either be found in the Hamr or in the Óðr. Which one it is depends on what definition of the astral you choose to pick. The Óðr is similar to a mental body, and Hamr to an astral body.

Looking at the Óðr first, it is a projection of the mind and spirit from the physical and energetic. This type of projection has no limit other than the rate of the energetic vibrational of your spirit. Mental projections such as these are typically achieved by mental focus shifts, perceptual shifts and so forth. They are not to be confused with other type of projection traditionally labelled as 'astral projection', which belong to a different category and are more akin to complete separation from the body. In these types of projections both the mind/spirit AND the entire energetic body are separated from the physical. This type of projection is characterised by the physical body going inert, very cold, and pale in complexion. It is also characterised as being very 'dangerous' as it allows the usurpation of the body taken by foreign agents whilst the Self is loose. In terms of the Norse Self, the mental type of 'astral projection' is the projection of the Óðr, and the more traditional type of 'astral' projection is the projection of the Hamr.

Having established the various bodies, we are dealing with, we can now turn to the question at hand. Keeping in mind that Megin is a substance rather than an energy per se, you should see across all the bodies a type of solidification. By circulating

Megin we are adding substance to our various 'bodies' which gives them the solidity they need to fully form.

It may be of interest to note that Megin has certain specific effects on each of the individual parts of the Self:

- In the Lik (physical body) it will heal and repair as a default behaviour.

- In the Hamr (etheric body) it will reform and strengthen the energy pathways and organs. It will also strengthen the energetic reserves and their storage capacity. Since the Hamr absorbs all the non-physical damage before it manifests physically, the stronger it is the better.

- In the Sal it will help with its formation and enable use of emotional energy generated by the physical rather than allowing it to be siphoned off by 'the thieves'. It also enhances fluidity of the Sal and the natural energetic absorption abilities it possesses.

- In the Hugr it quickens logical and thinking capabilities, as well as stretching them out. An essential ingredient to expanding consciousness.

- In the Minni it will grow memory stores, add power to the processes needed to store, retrieve and manipulate both physical and non-physical memories. A form of memory system quickening occurs. Recollection is strengthened. You will remember things more vividly and with more accuracy.

- In the Óðr it expands both the spirit and

the senses, which in turn is used to feed our spirits and empower them. It also serves to solidify the spirit and give it stability and consistency.

- In the Önd it awakens it, allowing it to flow through the whole Self and expand it. It is an essential component of the Önd itself.

- In the Fylgja it powers the Fylgja's abilities and functions, assists with the inter dimensional memory transfers, with faring forth (the projection of Flygja), connecting with the Kin-Fylgja (family / ancestral Fylgja), weaving of the personal Ørlǫg, and carrying out tasks you might send it on.

- In the Hamingja itself it has just as many functions – for those of you who want to learn more, the BoO[1] will give you more info.

Considering the above outline, you will find that the Megin and its properties are vital to all parts of the Self. Operating as a parallel function, it also serves to enable the flow of power and information across all the parts of the Self. Through this, harmonisation and consolidation of the parts of the Self into a self-sustaining organism across both physical and non-physical levels of reality is achieved. The stronger the Megin, the more powerful the Önd, the greater the abilities and reach of conscious awareness and, ultimately, the easier it is for the Self to maintain itself both in this life and into the next.

17. MY PSYCHIC ABILITIES HAVE INCREASED WHEN USING STAGE 1 AND 6 PRACTICES, HOW CAN I MAKE THIS EVEN MORE EFFECTIVE?

An interesting question, not least given that 'psychic' can mean different things to different people. Broadly speaking, most people define the psychic as being an extension of the usual or typical range of perceptual abilities (I'm avoiding the use of the term 'normal' since those extended perceptions ARE normal for mankind. We are just used to functioning in sub-normal capacity. This explains why they appear more than normal when we experience a perfectly normal functioning). The best terminology for these would be clair-voyance, clair-audiance, clair-feeling, clair-knowing, and sensing. The first three are easy to link back into our perception of enhanced senses of sight, hearing and touch. Clair-knowing is a bit trickier since it is the sixth sense; also termed 'the sense of spirit'. It is often confused with clair-feeling due to feeling and sensing being so alike. The best way to differentiate between the two is to remember that feeling is linked to touch, you need to make contact physically or energetically with something in order to feel it. Sensing does not have this restriction. You can pick up on information from as far and wide as your spirit is able to expand. This is strongly linked into what we in the modern day and age talk about in relation to 'intuitive knowing', but is also far more precise and direct. Sensing is not only a perceptual sense but an active one too.

Other definitions include some obscure skill sets such as materialisation, projections of various parts of the self and influencing things using non-physical means. As you can see there is a lot of room for mis-interpreting what exactly the term 'psychic' means. This is one of the root causes of so much mis-understanding and confusion when discussing such topics. Since it belongs to the domain of Seidr we're going to leave it there and focus on the aspects specific to Galdr and which aimed at enhancing perceptions.

By driving Megin into the eyes (the physical eyes) it will effect the energetic blueprint for the eye and enhance vision to include more and more of the physical reality we live in and move them to perceive the subtler side of the world around us (the energetic). Once both types of perception are fully functional, you will have gained the full sight in Midgard. This is what our vision was always meant to be. You can enhance these effects by building the Megin from energies of the runes ᚠ Fé (Fehu), ᛞ Dagur (Dagaz) and ᛗ Maður (Mannaz). Fill the Hamingja with them,

THEN infuse the eyes with the resulting Megin. IF AT ANY POINT IN TIME, you feel pressure in the eyes IMMEDIATELY empty the Megin from them and drive it back into the Hamingja; effectively unwinding the process. Pressure indicates energetic strain, ignore it and you will cause damage which can harm the physical eye too. Do not take risks with your vision! Keep it slow and steady. Keep things safe and manageable. Read your body and the messages it flags up for you. Respond to those promptly and responsibly. Give the eyes time to adapt to the Megin and give your conscious awareness time to adapt to the new perceptions. Work with your Self, do not force it or work against it. Respect it.

The same can be achieved with the other senses as well. The only difference is that for hearing you generate the Megin from ᚠ Óss (Ansuz) and ↑ Týr (Tiwaz) (ever wondered why there is a large telecoms company in the US with A and T in their name?). Once the Megin has been generated, imbue your inner ears with it and will it to enhance your hearing. Finally, for the sense of touch, use ᚱ Lögur (Laguz) and ✕ Gjöf (Gebo), imbue the resulting Megin in your skin.

As for the other senses and the sensing itself, these subjects will be dealt in later works that focus on the Óðr.

The few practices outlined above will enable you to greatly enhance your perceptions and push them a step at a time beyond the physical.

Expanding them into the other nine worlds will be extensively covered in a future publication.

18. I'VE NOTICED SINCE REGULAR PRACTICE WITH THE TECHNIQUES I HAVE BECOME ABLE TO COMPLETED SLIP OUT OF BODY PRACTICALLY AS SOON AS I REST WHEREAS BEFORE I COULDN'T DO IT NO MATTER WHAT TECHNIQUE I USED, HOW COMES?

This can happen, especially in the beginning. The reason for it is simple. When you charge up with Megin, once there is nothing major to heal physically and no Ørlǫg to weave, it will (unless redirected) automatically flow into other parts of the Self to strengthen those which are the weakest first. As these reserves increase, abilities which you have had since birth will get the fuel needed to activate. Then spontaneous projections can occur. The best thing to do is to just observe your immediate surroundings and your body from the projected Self's perspective then step back into the body. What this achieves is a type of loosening of the bonding material which 'glues' the physical and non-physical parts of the Self together, as well as allowing conscious awareness to realise that it is more than just the physical body.

There is a temptation when having such experiences to go explore, run about, float about and so forth. This is not recommended. The gradual stretching is what you need to achieve for long-term awakening of this ability. If you start wandering off and floating about the place once you get pulled back into the physical you will get stuck twice as strongly. The pull back is an instinctive response for survival of the physical body. Remember it has millions upon millions of tiny sparks of consciousness within itself which rely on your entire being to live. When you separate out, all of these micro-sparks of consciousness feel threatened, their very existence at risk, and they will pull you back with an instinct for survival. It is very likely that they will outmatch your will or ability to resist. By gradually relaxing this pull, both your own conscious mind and the countless 'micro-consciousness' existing in your body will realise that there is nothing to fear, that their existence is not being threatened by this separation. This will make the process easier and more natural in the long term. You are in effect sacrificing a few minutes of fun now for a lifetime of it later on.

Just keep feeding the other parts of the Self with Megin. Take it slow and steady. You will master the ability more and more until it becomes second nature.

19. What is the difference between Norse mysticism and Seidr (shammanism, prophetic seeing or trance work)? How about worship and what the Norse priesthood do?

Another fascinating question. It is important to understand the difference and finer points in between Seidr and runic mysticism (including Galdr).

Seidr is aligned with the arts of Vanaheim (Norse world of nature and natural forces) and the primordials, it is focussed on what is typically called shamanism and very much so on prophecy.

The Norns (cosmic Völva or Prophetess) are the link in the cosmic expression of the arts of Seidr. It is no surprise that the Norns are the ones shaping the Wyrd (fate) of everyone and everything in creation. The Völva have such incredible powers of vision across timelines that even Oðin goes to Helheim (Norse world of the dead) to wake a Völva to find out what is due to happen to Baldur (his son) prior to his death.

Seidr can be respectfully thought of as an 'art', you need the skill, the instinct, the perception and various kinds of sensitivities to be able to use and master this 'art'. Either you have the skill or potential for it or not. Of course some can train for Seidr but never will a trained individual be even remotely skilled as someone who has the natural affinity for it. It requires delicacy, instinctive intuition and 'doing because it just felt right' which is most akin to the feminine way of thinking. Hence, traditionally this was only taught to women. However, Oðin and other men did learn Seidr just as Freya and other women learnt Galdr. It seems more to do with an ability to shift the mind and associated perceptive mechanisms into the correct pattern rather than a gender lock as such (with the exception of their deepest mastery).

Runic Mysticism, on the other hand, is aligned with Asgard and the realms beyond it. Its primary goal is the evolution of the Self, the realisation of divinity within and then the shaping of creation. It is heavily reliant on the runes in order to tap into cosmic forces and powers and it is completely independent of spirits, gods, all external entities. All you need for it are the runes, practice and knowledge (DNA).

Rather than being an 'art', Galdr is rightfully thought of as a 'science'. By studying Galdr, especially High Galdr you will see that there are very specific methods producing set results. You select a particular rune, use it in the specified manner, and unleash it on a specific level of creation to gain a required effect.

You can always look at the runes, their use and their target(s) to deduct the exact effect(s) they will have (assuming proper use). This logic and patterning is why Galdr was typically taught to men, as it flows very naturally with the masculine way of thinking.

Seidr and Galdr were at certain points in time combined due to the characteristics of each system: Seidr manifests, shapes and leads to perception of powers and energies, whereas Galdr creates, precipitates and dynamises them. Seidr is downwards flowing and Galdr is upwards flowing. Hence the best way to think of their distinctions is to look at Galdr as the scientific manifestation of the higher knowledge of Asgard, and to consider Seidr as that coming down the traditional lines linked with the Völva. As such Seidr is more passive in application whereas Galdr is more active and direct. Galdr creates, Seidr shapes that which is created.

In answer to the worship question, Galdr was typically taught to the priests, it was seen as a holy sacred knowledge bestowed upon mankind by the Gods. However, it is important to look at the historical context, priesthood, worship and religion were never a dominant force where the Norse people. Their sharing of mead with the Gods was more akin to sharing a drink with a friend and honouring them at their table rather than religious worship as such. Religion as an established institution was absent to our ancestors. Ritual was a personal affair in between the individual, family, or clan and their respective God or Goddess.

APPENDIX

References & Footnotes

1. Frank A. Rúnaldrar (2016) - English. "The The Breath of Oðin Awakens – Secrets of the Önd, Hamingja & Norse Luck Unveiled". London: Bastian & West ISBN: 978-0-9955343-0-8

2. Karl G. Johansson, "Rígsþula och Codex Wormianus: Textens funktion ur ett kompilationsperspektiv," Alvíssmál 8 (1998) 67–84 – Downloaded from: http://userpage.fu-berlin.de/~alvismal/8rigr.pdf (Swedish) (English summary, p. 84).

CPSIA information can be obtained
at www.ICGtesting.com
Printed in the USA
BVOW08s1031261017
498718BV00001B/71/P